HOME ROCKANOMICS

54 PROJECTS AND RECIPES FOR STYLE ON THE EDGE

HOME ROCKANOMICS

54 PROJECTS AND RECIPES FOR STYLE ON THE EDGE

BY Heidi Minx

THOMAS DUNNE BOOKS

ST. MARTIN'S GRIFFIN

New York

THOMAS DUNNE BOOKS.
An imprint of St. Martin's Press.

HOME ROCKANOMICS. Copyright © 2009 by Heidi Minx. All rights reserved.
Printed in the United States of America.
For information, address St. Martin's Press, 175 Fifth Avenue, New York, N.Y. 10010.

www.thomasdunnebooks.com
www.stmartins.com
Book design by Jonathan Bennett
All tutorial photos by Eric Vogel.
All photos not credited are from the author's personal collection.
Vegan bike tire belt project and photos courtesy of MollyPop.

Library of Congress Cataloging-in-Publication Data
Minx, Heidi.
    Home rockanomics: 54 projects and recipes for style on the edge/Heidi Minx.—
1st ed.
        p. cm.
    ISBN 978-0-312-53755-5
    1. Handicraft. 2. Clothing and dress—Remaking. 3. Cookery. I. Title.
    TT157 .M53 2009
    745.5—dc22
                                                    2009017062

First Edition: November 2009

WHAT'S IN HERE

Rankin' Roger, minx, and Andy

minx and HR

Joey, minx, and Dave

Jasta, Stigma, Armand, minx, Jimmy, and Jorge

minx, Stigma, and Bif

Cuz, minx, and Freddy

minx and Zoli

Randy, minx, and Lou backstage

minx, Lars, and Cuz
Courtesy of Samma Jamma

With Sick of It All
Courtesy of Rudy DeDoncker

THIS BOOK IS DEDICATED to a lot of people, because so many people have been important in my life. Special thanks to my dad, for teaching me rhetoric, kindness, and to stand on my own two feet. To my brothers, Tad and Sab, for seeing me, unconditionally, through so many ups and downs. To Pete and Mei, for being two of the most genuine and supportive friends I've ever had. To Freddy and Joe and the Black N Blue family, for all their efforts in keeping our scene alive. To all the members of PRD, no one could ask for a better "family." To Heidi Van Horne, Theo, Sonya, and all the board "experts," for offering their advice and time. To Gunns, Bob, Laura, Steph Twinkie Chan, Eric, Diane, Jules, Gogo, Kimpulsive, Lou, Jenny/Trophy Queen, Elise/Hellkats-LA, Red, DirtyRottenLove, and all the bands that over the years have made the music that is the soundtrack to my life.

INTRODUCTION

For the kids, for the crafters, for the punk-in-spirit, for the people who do it themselves.

DIY is such a huge "business" today, and frankly, so is punk—but they just don't seem to be seen together. This is a fun book that helps visually sanctify the inseparable union of punk rock and DIY.

DIY is nothing new. In fact, it is pretty much how most things in this world were created. But it has a special home within punk, one where it still can't be beaten back by slick music videos or "distressed" denim in every store in the mall.

Punk rock, which we could call the bastard stepchild to rock and roll, has always had to find its way on its own: Your neighborhood hairdresser did not understand that you wanted blue hair; bands recorded in their garages with a tape recorder from RadioShack; clothing was re-created from thrift-store scores; and shows were usually in the most rundown clubs in the worst areas. Yet despite all those odds, as a whole, punk has kicked its way forward and is a unifying voice worldwide.

Punk and all its manifestations are born from necessity and a desire to do something differently. If it doesn't exist the way you want it, well, then make it.

That is what you'll find in this book, which was written purely because of the great response, feedback, and support from members on my community DIY site, Punk Rock Domestics. There are some home-styling tips on a budget, some "anti-fashion" tips and tricks, and a lot of random pointers—because, well face it, we usually figure this stuff out by accident! I've gotten where I am today (which would be, bringing you this book by your request!) because I've done things myself, questioned everything, and worked hard.

I want this book to inspire you to create your own look, to make it fun to shop at bargain stores, and to make your space yours without breaking the bank.

I was born in Baltimore, and it was there, at thirteen, that I discovered punk. I never had too many friends, and the few I did have definitely left my parents disappointed. It was those early friends who turned me on to punk. I remember the first day my friend Greg had me come to his house after school and made me mix tapes. My first ones were GI, UK Subs, Agnostic Front, Warzone, Minor Threat, and Grey March.

I began racking the local record stores, where if I was lucky I would find Black Flag, White Flag—I looked for anything with flyer art on the cover. I wound up in art school. Luckily, there was an art magnet high school in Baltimore—if not, I doubt I would have finished. I bleached my hair, I dyed it black, and I'd go downtown to hang out. As friends got old enough to drive, I'd go to D.C. on the weekends to see shows at the old 9:30 Club. Whether it was the Toasters, Bad Brains, or Lucy Brown, I jumped at every opportunity to go out.

R.I.P. CBGB

I worked hard to go to college with as many scholarships as possible. I painted and was entrenched in art. I loved the fact that I could question and challenge in that environment. Schools took me to Chicago, Milwaukee, and, later, Brighton in the U.K. Wherever I went, I found like-minded people in the punk, ska, mod, and psychobilly scenes. I always seemed to trip into things. I first learned about the band Demented Are Go because I lived with one of the member's brothers. I got my first bartending gig in the U.K. because the guys from Bad Manners were playing and recommended me to the club owner. I'd spend weekends camping at scooter rallies or going to gigs in London, and pushed my way through my classes with whatever energy I had left.

I lived in Glasgow for a while, moved back to Baltimore, and later to New York. It was in New York that I realized my life was inseparable from my roots. Even though I consulted in marketing for large companies by day, my work ethics, the type of things I was doing, always seemed to take me straight back to punk and DIY.

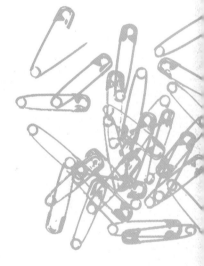

In 2001, I started a licensed line called Franky & Minx, based off of tattoo art. I worked hard to push that line forward (without any funding but my own!), and it saw some brief success but also became a painful reminder to me of how hard it is to believe and push forward when most business-people care only about their bottom line. In 2005, I started Punk Rock Domestics (PRD), really as a place to share things. So many of my friends were musicians, and I wanted to share what they'd learned and what I'd learned, with other cool, crafty people. PRD started off as a MySpace page, and once we stepped up to our own Web site with an interactive message board, we crashed our server in the first six weeks! Since then, PunkRockDomestics .com has become a cult, an underground phenomenon, and a safe and lively haven for alternative culture, with members even organizing their own local PRD meet-ups. I wanted people to see that the punk lifestyle doesn't have to be degenerate or angry but positive, questioning, and firm in its ethics. As Joe Strummer said, *"Punk rock is exemplary manners towards your fellow human being."*

I had started studying Buddhism back in 2000. Dharma (its teachings) fueled me and resonated with my punk nature to question, to care for others, to stand firm in beliefs, and to find alternative ways to do things. I also encourage anyone reading this book to check out Built on Respect (www.builtonrespect.com), a charity I started so I can help teach people around the world skills that can make a difference in communities. It embodies everything I am today. Noah Levine defined this spirit perfectly in his book, *Dharma Punx*—he called it "Against the Stream": It's not always easy to do the right thing; it's easy to run with the crowd, overlook something, and slip into "the grind." It takes something more to question, to look (not overlook), to speak your mind, to identify and rectify injustices, and be an individual.

PRD's Home Rockanomics is dedicated to living against the stream: looking at things in different ways, finding purpose in what you do, being creative (it fuels your soul), and finding a way to do something good every day—whether it's recycling, helping a friend, or opening your mind to something new. Enjoy!

STREET STYLE

PUNK IS TRULY ITS OWN STYLE. Like everything in true punk, it's born out of DIY, distaste for the mainstream offerings, the 'anti' attitude - think Social Distortion's 'Anti-Fashion' - anti mall 'rubber stamp fashion' and anti-mass consumerism.

From the Sex Pistols, to Duane Peters, to Rancid's Lars Frederiksen, deconstruction and destruction reign.

My personal closet has quite a few items that I love, usually the ones I've found and modified, and said, **"That is SO ugly, it's cool."** Plaids, stripes, distraught textures, these are a few of my favorite things.

Patches, snaps, paint, bleach, safety pins, and zippers - all are staples of the punk look, but it is the wearer's unique ability to make something from nothing and to express themselves - and wear it with pride - that makes this style one that is truly unique.

SEXY SWEATERS

Oversize sweaters can become simply sexy
with shears, pins, and a little patience.

MY FAVORITE "CLOTHING STORE" was my father's closet. Much to his chagrin, I'd frequently help myself to his sweaters, especially the old worn ones. Unfortunately, I was a small and he was an XL. I can't tell you the number of times I'd solve that problem by washing his sweaters in hot water and putting them in the dryer. He was NONE too impressed. To this day, I love sweaters, but usually not the ones I see in the stores. I still prefer the older ones, a simple wool crewneck, but I don't always want to look like a boy wearing one. About two years ago I began to tailor my oversize sweaters so I could feel at least slightly like a girl, even in the New York winters.

WHAT YOU'LL NEED:

- A sweater that is too big (one with a tighter knit that can be sewn with a sewing machine)

- Good cutting shears or pinking shears

- Straight pins

- Sewing machine

- Trim, if you're feeling decorative

- A friend to help fit the sweater on you

1. Put the sweater on and, following the seams, have your friend carefully use the straight pins to fit it to you—up the sides, along the bottom of the arms, anywhere it is baggy.

2. Once you wiggle out of it, check that the pins seem even and grab your scissors. Cut away the excess fabric, about $\frac{1}{4}$ inch away from the pins.

3. Then use your sewing machine to sew back up the sides. Personally I leave the sweater seams raw and exposed on the outside. I recommend at least three runs, to make sure that the edges are well put back together.

4. For this sweater, I decided to make a lower neck and used some trim to finish off the front. To stop it from fraying, I just sewed around the cutout neck several times.

I've washed this in the machine numerous times, and it has yet to fray past the stitching.

BLEACH PEN DENIM

Save the stencils and go freehand.
Denim (preferably dark!) is your easiest fabric to modify.

WHAT YOU'LL NEED:

- Clorox Bleach Pen (around $3.50 from any drugstore)
- Scrap paper
- Water-soluble marker
- Your canvas—a denim jacket or jeans

1. Sketch out your pattern or design with a simple water-based marker directly on the fabric.

2. Test your bleach pen on a piece of paper so you get a good clean line of bleach gel with no bubbles or blobs.

3. Once you get a good flow, begin drawing on your fabric. Depending on how dark your denim is, the gel may need to sit for a longer period of time. Just keep your eye on it; you'll notice as it is lightening.

4. Make sure to rinse with cold water when you are done (I usually let cold water run over it in the kitchen sink for about 5 minutes), and wash for the first time with rags or on its own, so you don't get bleach on your other items!

TIP: Once you've finished your item and it's been properly washed, you may want to consider using RIT Dye to overdye the garment. Red RIT works well on denim—especially when you've bleached in flames!

Courtesy of Scott Clinton

MAKE YOUR T-SHIRTS WORK FOR YOU

Two of my good girlfriends—the lovely Jenny Gunns of Dirty Mary and the inspiring Bif Naked—taught me these tricks. As Bif used to say, she didn't want to show if she was "shvitzing" on stage.

WHAT YOU'LL NEED:

All you need are . . .

- Scissors
- safety pins
- a T-shirt

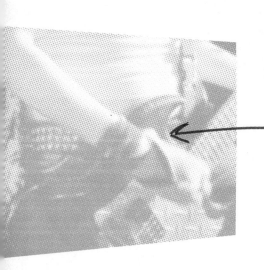

When you want to modify a T-shirt, save the bottom edging, wrap it around your wrist a few times, and avoid wearing another trendy rash guard.

For sweat-free simplicity, trim up from the armpit to the side of the collar diagonally.

Beauty: on the lam!

* Keep Preperation H PADS in the FRIDGE. ON A MORNING WHEN YOUR UNDEREYES ARE too PUFFY to bear — cut ONE PAD in half — and put both halves under your eyes — they'll stick on their own. leave them on for about 3 minutes & you're good to go — (NOTE: DO NOT put over your WHOLE EYE!)

* SAVE your old t-shirt scraps to make 2" x 6" strips. TAKE sections of hair & roll them around the strip — then tie off in one tie -- Quicker than rollers — EASIER to sleep in!

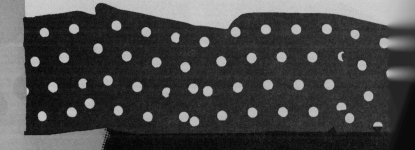

SIMPLE STENCILS

STENCILS ARE GREAT FOR ANYTHING – walls, furniture, sidewalks, and, of course, clothing. Their negative spaces and blocky designs are a project in themselves or a great starter for a blank canvas!

WHAT YOU'LL NEED:

- 1 roll contact paper (clear is best; around $3 at any grocery store)

- 1 good X-Acto knife

- 1 bottle strong bleach (the stuff at the hardware store is often better than Clorox)

- 1 small spray bottle with a mist setting

- Paper towels or paper napkins

- Clothing you want to improve (denim works well; Dickies do not).

continued...

1. Choose a simple negative-space stencil design. Using an X-Acto, cut it out of contact paper. Make 2 or 3 copies of the stencil if you are going to use it multiple times on one garment.

2. Peel the backing off and place your stencil on a tee or jeans. (Cotton is easier to bleach than synthetic fabrics.)

3. Put some bleach in a spray bottle. (I find bleach from the hardware store is stronger than bleach you get for laundry at a grocery store.)

4. Mist your bleach over the stencil pattern. You can blot the excess bleach off the contact paper with a paper towel, quickly lift the stencil off the fabric and place it elsewhere, and mist again.

5. When the fabric lightens to the desired level, throw the item in a cold wash in the washing machine. Don't wash other items with the ones you've just bleached!

NOTE: Spray paint also works
well with stencils. (Krylon holds up
very well in the washing machine!)

Here's a pair of jeans done with a more complex stencil.

REVIVING OLD PANTS

TOO SHORT? Bell bottoms? It's really easy to adjust pant bottoms to fit your current personal style. You don't have to be a sewing genius or spend a fortune at the tailor if you have a few fabric scraps and some hardware or zippers.

TO LENGTHEN PANTS, YOU'LL NEED:

- Sewing machine
- About ¼-yard fabric
- Straight pins

This project isn't too rocket science; it's pretty simple.

1. Take your fabric and hold it up to the bottom of your pants.

2. Cut the fabric wide enough to wrap all the way around the bottom of the pant leg, and long enough to make your pants the length you desire.

3. Pin the fabric in place with straight pins. I find it's easier to have the two fabric ends join on the inside pants' leg seam.

4. If you can, remove the tray on your machine so the sewing area is small enough to fit the "cuff" of the pants around the platen.

5. Just begin to sew. I don't stop; I just keep sewing in a circle, rotating the pants until I've sewed all the fabric on and closed up the ends of the scrap fabric.

If you want to peg your pants ('cuz let's face it, bell bottoms were NEVER punk!), then just grab some hardware. and turn to the next page...

TO PEG YOUR PANTS, YOU'LL NEED:

- 2 zippers (between 6"--10", depending on your preference/measurements)
- Embroidery floss (1 packet; choose a cool color!)
- Scissors
- 1 strong needle
- Straight pins
- A sewing machine is helpful but not necessary

1. Start by putting your pants on and marking the outside seams where you want the tapering to begin (usually lower calf).

2. Hold your zipper up to that marked point to make sure it is long enough

3. Pants back off!

4. Using good shears, cut directly into the pants' outside seam, up to the point you marked.

5. Next, cut away some of the extra fabric, taking care to cut equal amounts on either side of your original cut. Your finished cuts should make it look like you've cut out a very long upside-down **V** out of the outside seam.

6. Using straight pins, pin your zipper on the outside of the pants to close that open area. Make sure to try your pants on to make sure they fit. If you have pegged them supertight, just unzip the zipper to get your feet through, then rezip to make sure the legs are sitting properly and are even on both sides!

7. Pants off again! Use your needle and embroidery floss to sew the zipper onto the fabric. I use **X** stitches and simple "under and over" stitching. If you do have a sewing machine, you can sew the zipper to the fabric that way first, then use the floss to reinforce it.

TIP: You don't just have to use zippers! Take a look at the fastener hooks I used on this pair!

WINTER-TO-SUMMER CROP TOP

Convert a **boring** button-up to a flirty crop.

THIS DESPERATE LITTLE NUMBER was given to me by the lovely pinup model, Heidi Van Horne. She had picked it up at Kmart of all places; it's part of the Kathie Lee line! She joked that she got it when polka dots were hard to find. I promised, as a favor for all her help on the PRD boards, that I would take it as a personal challenge to make it wearable!

WHAT YOU'LL NEED:

- Scissors
- 4 safety pins (1" work best!)
- About 1 yard of trim (your choice!)
- Sewing machine
- Straight pins
- A button-up shirt that desperately needs a makeover

1. Put the shirt on and mark the length you want, anywhere from below the bust to just above the belly button.

2. Take the shirt off, lay it flat, and cut across that line, but **DON'T** cut off the button and buttonhole strip! (Those will be your ties.)

3. Next, cut around the armholes, just inside the armhole seam.

4. The trim is optional. If you have a sewing machine, use straight pins to put your ribbon in place—running from the bottom of the "ties" on both sides and up and around the exposed edges—then sew in place.

5. Chances are you're going to need to improvise some darts at the bustline. If there's extra fabric that's gapping, fold it over on itself. Safety pins are easy to use; just fold over the fabric to create a dart and pin. If you want to be fancy, you could sew it in place. Or just leave it!

MAKE-YOUR-OWN FELT PATCHES

Use felt scraps and embroidery floss
to make simple, bright patches.

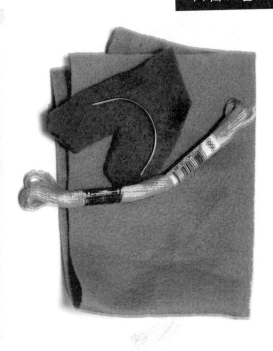

WHAT YOU'LL NEED:

- Felt scraps in different colors (a 12" x 10" piece is usually less than $1 at a craft or fabric store)

- Fun colors of embroidery floss

- A needle you can thread with the floss

- Scissors

1. Create a simple design—a skull, stars, hearts, dice, a simple band logo (like, Black Flag simple!).

2. Use 1 piece of felt as your background and the other colors to create your design.

3. Sew the pieces onto the background, then sew on to whatever you want!

I just sewed a super simple skull
onto a pair of gloves I had lying around.

Polish Docs to a Super Shine

* To get a high polish on docs, use a soft cloth to put a generous layer of matching Kiwi polish on the boot.

- Then, use a Zippo about 2 inches away from the boot to lightly heat the wax into the leather - the flame tip should just "kiss" the leather as you pass it over the surface.

- Use an old nylon stocking to polish off the wax for a super "Military" shine.

INSTANT BELT LOOPS

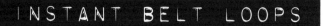

SOME THINGS just don't have the right belt loops—like Dickies (they're too small)—and some skirts don't have them at all.

It's supereasy to get around: Grab 4 large kilt pins and affix them to the outside waistband. The larger kilt pins can even fit a 3-row pyramid stud belt!

STUDS AND SPIKES

THOUGH THERE ARE GREAT SITES like studsandspikes.com, it can still get a bit pricey to add metal to a jacket. Found items can be just as fun.

WHAT YOU'LL NEED:

- Old Bic Lighters
- Pliers
- Sandpaper (fine-grain is OK)
- Bottle caps (not bent from opening)
- Awl and hammer
- Thread and needle

1. You can easily sand the logo off a metal bottle cap.

2. Using an awl and a hammer, poke two "button-style" holes in the tops (like buttonholes) and sew on to a garment.

3. The silver tabs in lighters are an easy way to get a "bound" metal edge on cuffs and lapels. Using pliers, pry the silver part off an old lighter. Then clamp it over the edge of the fabric.

TIP: The lighter tabs work well on hat brims as well!

VEGAN BIKE TIRE BELT

MollyPop from the PRD boards posted this tutorial. I loved it so much, I asked her if we could include it in the book. All pictures and instructions are from her!

THIS IS AN EASY WAY to make a non-leather studded belt that's cheaper than buying one!

WHAT YOU'LL NEED:

- A bicycle tube*
- Scissors**
- Studs
- A marker that will show up on black tubing (optional)
- Something to push down the prongs of the studs with (a screwdriver or scissors work)

* To find a busted bicycle tube, you could probably go to a bike shop near you and look in the dumpster or ask if they have any unfixable tubes lying around.

** If you don't have a pair of **heavy-duty** scissors, buy them. It's an investment.

1. First, take your bicycle tube and cut it across so it's not in a circle.

2. Now cut it along one of the lines so it turns into a flat length of rubber. The lines are a really good guide for cutting a straight line. It'll probably be pretty icky on the inside.

3. Next, trim the rubber so it's the width you want for your belt. But beware: You don't want to have to stud around the nozzle. Make sure that it's not included in your width.

4. After you've done that, you can wash off the ickies if you want.

5. To make sure your width is how you want it, try it on and pull it through your belt loops.

6. Mine is a little big for my loops, so I'm going to trim it down a little.

continued...

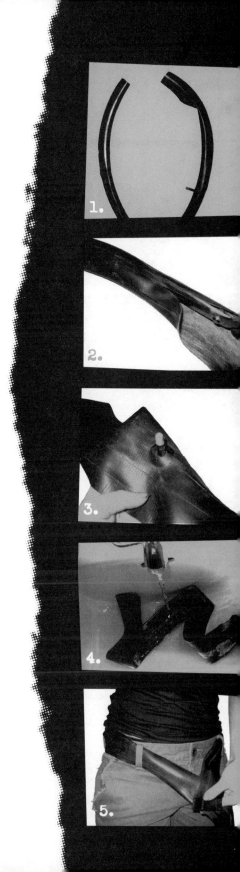

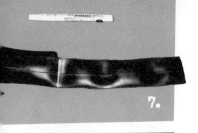

7.

8a.

8b.

9/10.

11.

12.

7. After you've gotten the right width, while it's still through your belt loops mark where you want your studs to end/start and also where you need to trim it if it's too long. Remember to leave enough room at each end unstudded so you can tighten and loosen it. You can always add more studs at the end after you've dealt with the buckle.

8. And now, once it's marked and trimmed, you can start to stud. It doesn't matter how you arrange your studs.

9. Now try it on.

10. From here you should be able to tell where you want the holes to be to tighten/loosen it. If you have a belt buckle, you can add that on there. If not, you can use studs as buttons.

11. So, add studs down the middle of one end like so: I did three to start.

12. Try it on again: I already had one huge hole, which was why the tube was unusable, so I decided to make that my first hole.

13.

14.

15.

13. Take it off and line up the non-button-stud end to the button-stud one and mark dots so when you cut the holes, they'll line up with the studs.

14. Cut little crosses where you marked the dots.

15. And the studs should go in like this.

16. Line them all up: It works! Now you can make any minor adjustments, like adding more studs, trimming the ends, or adding more holes.

17. Once you have all that taken care of, you're done! You can adjust how tight it is by lining up different holes with different studs. I would also recommend reinforcing it with a safety pin; sometimes studs don't make the greatest buttons.

The average vegan studded belt can be over $20, while making it this way (assuming you already own scissors) is only the cost of studs. A bag of 100 standard $\frac{1}{2}$-pyramid studs costs $3.40, not including shipping (from CrustPunks.com). Yay!

16.

17.

PATTERNS AND PRINTS

IN ART SCHOOL, collagraph prints were my favorite projects. They didn't require as many chemicals and, to me, were one of the forms of printmaking that had the most varied results—you **NEVER** knew what your finished print would look like. Collagraphs can be a great way to add texture and colors, and, ultimately, after use, they become a piece of art on their own!

A collagraph print is made by placing different items onto a boardlike surface, affixing them, and then inking on the textured surfaces and using it as a print template.

WHAT YOU'LL NEED:

- Cardboard canvas (available from any art store)
- Found items (think zippers, safety pins, strings)
- Modge Podge (available at craft/art stores; about $5)
- Textile paints (available at craft/art stores)
- Hot-glue gun and about 5 glue sticks
- Paintbrushes
- Iron
- T-shirt to print on

1. With your brush, coat your canvas with two layers of Modge Podge (MP) or a similar acrylic substance, like gesso.

2. Choose your found items and begin to glue them onto the board (either with MP or your hot-glue gun). You will want to keep a fairly uniform height with the items, as you will be pressing this by hand, not through a printing press. The uniform height of the items will help get an even print area.

3. Use your MP or gesso to create a sealing layer over your items once you have them affixed. Let it dry (this may take up to an hour if you used a lot of found items).

4. Drizzle hot glue all over the dried collagraph; this helps hold down the items and also creates cool shapes and textures. Let glue dry.

continued...

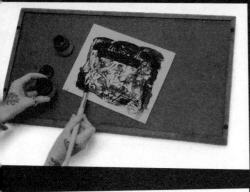

5. Using brushes, your fingers, whatever, begin to apply your fabric paints over the raised areas. Play around with paint thickness and colors.

6. Lay your shirt, jeans, denim-jacket back (whatever you are applying your design to) out on the floor.

7. Lay your collagraph board facedown on the fabric and apply pressure—use your hands, stand on it, whatever you deem fit!

8. Lift up your collagraph and allow your fabric to dry. When it's dry, place a scrap of fabric over it and iron to set the paint.

You can use your collagraph again and again. It gains more and more personality each time you use it!

TIP: They look cool hanging on the wall as art!

WINDY SPRING SCARF

SCARVES ARE HANDS DOWN one of my favorite accessories. On spring and summer nights, I love them—go to a concert, stuff one in your bag, be warm on the way home hours later. When I was in India this past year, there was so much fun cotton plaid, I wound up grabbing a lot of it. When I got home I had to find ways to use it.

TO MAKE A FUN SCARF THAT WON'T BLOW IN YOUR FACE OR DOWN THE STREET, YOU'LL NEED:

- About a yard of fun fabric
- Needle and thread
- About 3 feet of a lightweight chain

1. Quite simply, fold your fabric in half lengthwise and sew up the open sides. Flip it inside out, so the seam is on the inside and, if you want to, iron it. You'll give your scarf shape and make the next step easier.

2. Next, divide your chain in half (scissors will work if it's lightweight chain); you'll need some for both ends of the scarf.

3. To finish off the ends, begin to roll the fabric ends, tucking under the exposed fabric hem-like. As you roll and whipstitch your raw ends, sew the chain on to it. (I used about 3 whip stitches for every link of chain.) The final item will have the chain exposed on the outside (not sewn into the roll)!

Works like a charm and looks supercute with plaid cotton!

HOME HELP

I WAS AN ART STUDENT. I studied it at an
art magnet high school and then I worked my way
through several art colleges. Early on, I looked
at everything as a "project." How could I make this
from that, and for no money? Art school and punk
rock pretty much had the same ethos: Figure it out,
make it, do it yourself. I've lived all over the world,
in so many cities, in so many apartments. As I think
back, I remember the milk-crate bookshelves, the
sheets-as-curtains, the yard sales, and, my personal
favorite, the trash scores . . .

The last weekend of the month is always the best to scour the streets for trash. Everyone's moving, and there's plenty they'll leave behind. I've had friends meet me on corners in the height of summer with a skateboard to try and move a 250-pound file cabinet back to my place (thanks Pete!), and in the dead of winter with a small handcart to move a steel locker chucked outside of a school (thanks Gogo!).

Today, late at night as I flip through the 700-plus channels on my TV, I see home shows. "Get this designer look"—blah, blah, blah. I live in a city: I like it urban; **I like things raw**; I like the textures of scraped paint. I firmly believe your home should be your sanctuary, where you can paint and play, and where it doesn't always have to be perfect or designer but is truly a reflection of who you are.

I've always got spray paint at hand, stencils, and a few tools. The projects in here are for people who **ARE** on a budget, who **AREN'T** happy with cookie cutter, and who do see the art and potential in everything. I suggest treating the next piece of trash you see like the back of your old leather jacket and having fun with it!

QUICK RACK

NEED AN EXTRA RACK, or some extra hanging space? This is a great fix in a pinch that a friend taught me.

WHAT YOU'LL NEED:

- 2 plastic soda caps
- A small saw (or sharp serrated knife)
- A cutting surface
- A $\frac{1}{2}$"-- to 1"-wide dowel rod
- 4 nails

1. Take one of the soda caps and, using a small saw, cut down one side of the cap so that it appears like a C instead of an O. A saw is best, but the plastic is soft, so if you're careful a knife will work in a pinch.

2. Take the second, uncut cap and use 2 nails to nail it into the wall at the height you want the rack.

3. Put one end of the rod into the cap and use that to measure where you will need the second cap "holder."

4. Nail the second cap into the wall, with the cut side facing upward. Again, 2 nails, so it won't want to spin or turn.

5. Then, just slide the dowel rod into the opening and voilà! Enough extra hanging space to make you feel like you've moved to a house in the 'burbs.

ANTIQUE CHARM

Down with the White Walls!

YOU KNOW THE DILEMMA: You move into a cool spot, one you think has character and charm, and before you move in the landlord runs in and whitewashes the place. Every bit of charm just went out the window with those two gallons of "Iron White Flat." No problem: With a little imagination, you can get the glamour of a bordello or the smoky seediness of an old-school tattoo parlor.

FOR BORDELLO CHARM, YOU'LL NEED:

- Polyurethane
- Silk flowers
- Paint brush or roller
- Staple gun (or hot- glue gun or small nails)
- Clear spray paint
- Paint roller and tray
- Newspaper as a drop cloth, in case you're messy!

1. Roll a single coat of polyurethane over those white walls. Don't worry too much about being even; Inconsistency adds to the charm.

2. Randomly staple (or hot glue or nail) the cut tops of flowers over the walls or near the corners.

3. Use the clear spray paint over the flowers to give them a shiny finish similar to the wall's.

continued...

- Clips from magazines, your favorite drawings, old postcards, or flash art!

- Polyurethane

- A small foam brush

- A paint roller and tray

- Newspaper or a drop cloth, in case you're messy!

1. Brush or roll a liberal amount of your polyure-thane on the walls. No need to be even; random coats will ensure an antiqued glow, similar to years of smoke and age that you can only find on good old flash.

2. Decide where you want to have the various images you've chosen on your walls.

3. Place your images directly onto the wet polyurethane; they should stick perfectly well.

4. Once the first coat has dried and your art is well adhered to the walls, use another coat of polyurethane to help "age" the images.

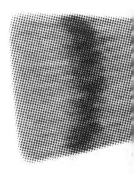

ANOTHER WAY AROUND WALLPAPER

Why pay for fancy flowery wallpaper when you can, well, avoid the gluey mess and do it for less?

WHAT YOU'LL NEED:

- Several yards of cheap lace, preferably with large negative areas and a flower pattern you like
- Several cans of spray paint (black is my favorite!)
- Base coat paint (have fun: think gold, silver, or a blood red!)
- A paint roller
- 2 small tacks
- A face mask of some sort
- Newspaper for the floor

1.

1. Paint the walls with your base color and go bold. (Remember: If you are using black to make your flower pattern, it will mute slightly.)

2. Once the paint has dried, use 2 small tacks and tack the top 2 corners of your lace onto your wall.

3. Tie SOMETHING on your face and shake your spray paint. Spray about 10 inches away from the wall, in fairly even, sweeping strokes.

4. When you've completed the "first pass," move the lace over and go again. Since it will never be "perfect," have fun overlapping and changing the directions of the lace as you spray.

3.

4.

ROAD WARRIOR WORK AREAS

Tires, some baby food jars, a nail gun, and some screws can totally rock out any space—and give YOU more space.

YOU'LL NEED:

- A regular car tire, cut in half (this may require heavy machinery; call someone who knows how to use it without losing fingers!)
- A piece of shelving or wood (about 6" wide and long enough to sit across the top of the tire)
- Nail gun
- 3 or 4 glass jars with metal tops
- 3 or 4 nuts and bolts
- 4 screws
- Screwdriver
- A power hand drill

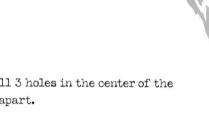

1. Starting with your ½ tire, drill 3 holes in the center of the treading area, about 5 inches apart.

2. Remove lids from jars and drill a hole in the center of each of the metal jar lids.

3. Using your nuts and bolts, affix the lids to the exterior, on the tire tread.

4. Using a nail gun or, if you don't have one, your drill, puncture 4 holes into one side of the tire. (These are the holes through which you will affix it to your wall, so space them evenly for optimal anchoring.)

5. Place your tire against the wall and level it; it should look like the smile in a smiley face.

6. Using your screws and screwdriver, affix the tire to the wall.

7. Now fill your jars with whatever you want and twist them back on to their lids.

8. Last, you'll need that shelf—the one you measured and cut! Just lay it across the top of the tire, and voilà! A neato storage area.

CD CASE PICTURE FRAMES

**Do some creative recycling
and decorate at the same time.**

- Hot-glue gun (4 glue sticks)
- CD jewel case (remove CD tray)
- Scissors
- Fabric scraps (four pieces, about 6" x 6" inches)
- Fun trimmings or ribbon (about 15")
- 2 pictures

1. Measure length and width of both the inside and outside panels of the jewel case; your 4 pieces of fabric will be used to cover these, and dimensions vary a bit.

2. Separate the jewel case carefully (you don't want to break the hinge!).

3. Cut your fabrics for each panel. I suggest some thicker wools or felts; they work better with the hot glue.

4. If you want to sew a picture to your fabric, make sure you sew it to the panel that fits the inside of the jewel case. You can use your trim here, add pins, anything you want to complete the picture panels before you put them in the frame.

5. Heat up your glue gun and put a liberal amount on your first panel. You'll need to do the edges and across the middle—then quickly lay your first panel of fabric on.

6. Repeat for all 4 panels.

7. Trim away any excess fabric with scissors.

8. Your last step is the outside trim—use your glue gun to affix it.

9. Put the frame back together by joining the 2 jewel case panels.

KEEP CRAFT-TIME CLEAN
Hot-glue guns rule for all sorts of things and are one of the cheapest things you can invest in to fix almost anything. The only setback (besides potential burns!) is that they're messy. If you're getting crafty, run to the bathroom first and find an empty toilet paper roll. Place the barrel of the glue gun into the roll (small glue guns will fit perfectly). Glue will drip into the tube, not on your work surface.

CUSTOMIZE YOUR SHEETS

FACE IT, it's not easy to find supercool sheets and duvet covers. It's supereasy, though, to make your own sets.

FOR A RAD BOUDOIR, YOU'LL NEED:

- 2 sheet sets (ideally one that includes fitted sheets, a flat sheet, and 2 pillowcases)

- Sewing machine and buttons (only if you are making the duvet version)

- Fabric paint and brushes

- Iron

- Scrap fabric

- Contact paper (or acetate, something to make a stencil with)

1. Choose a simple negative-space design, like cherries or skulls, and create your stencil (see the stencil tutorial on page 29). You may want to make a smaller version of the stencil for the edges of your pillowcases. Contact paper is a great stencil choice. Peel off the backing and place the sticky side on the fabric, and it will make for very clean lines!

2. If you don't usually sleep with a top sheet, sew the edges of the two flat sheets together to make your own duvet cover that will now match both of your fitted sheets and pillowcases. If you **DO** use a flat sheet, stencil across the tops of the sheets, so when you fold them over your blankets, you have a fun design showing.

3. Using your stencils, begin to stencil your designs with fabric paints. Use smaller versions of the stencils to paint the edges of your pillowcases.

4. When you're done stenciling and your paint is dry, make sure to set each design with an iron. Fabric paint needs to be heated in order not to rinse off in the wash. Put your iron on its highest setting and place some scrap fabric between your iron and the design on your sheets, so the paint does not smear!

5. If you sewed the 2 flat sheets together, find fun buttons to close off the bottom seam.

ANOTHER IDEA: Paint your stencils onto fun fabric scraps and sew them onto your duvet cover for a patched effect.

WINDOWPANES TO ART FRAMES

YOU'LL NEED:

- Masking tape
- Crystal Clear Packaging Tape
- Art print
- Old windowpane

1. Look for windowpanes that don't have broken glass. My favorites are old wooden ones with lots of texture.

2. Clean glass and choose a fun print that will "float" in the windowpane area.

3. Run strips of masking tape neatly and exactly down the inside edges of the back of your print. The masking tape will help protect the edges.

4. Then, run Crystal Clear Packaging Tape down the masking-taped areas of the print; the other part will lie directly on the glass.

5. Use an X-Acto to trim away excess tape.

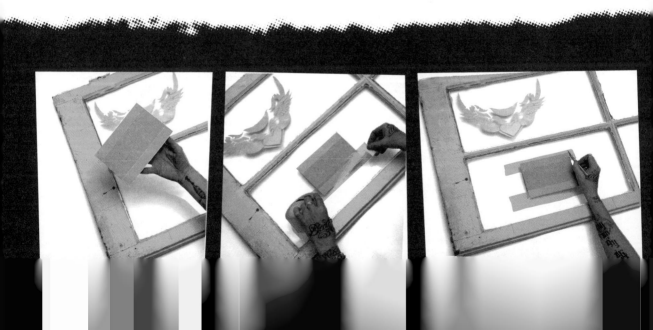

The print will stay put for quite a while; mine have lasted for well over five years without any touch-ups!

TRASH DIVE

Simply painting can make garbage great! I've found lockers, very ugly brown desks, piles of door frames . . . all sorts of things. Here are some before and after shots.

X-rays are expensive. If you're unfortunate enough to need one, you may as well get the most from it. Last time I broke a toe, I made it a point to go to a cheap X-ray clinic, where they let me have my X-ray to take back to my doctor myself. Once my doctor verified what we both knew (yup, it was broken), I asked if I could keep it.

This is where you can show off your injury and your stellar taste at the same time to all your guests. Use your X-ray as a lamp shade. Bending it in one direction can give it a sconcelike shape. If you break a couple of bones, follow the directions below.

YOU'LL NEED:

- X-rays
- Small lamp shade with a wire frame
- Stapler
- Scissors
- Acetate for alternate panels (I actually used 3M's Scotchlite in this one, which I had samples of from sourcing materials for Franky & Minx)
- Tape—think duct tape, electrical tape (I used 3M's retro-reflective tape here— again, from sourcing fashion materials)

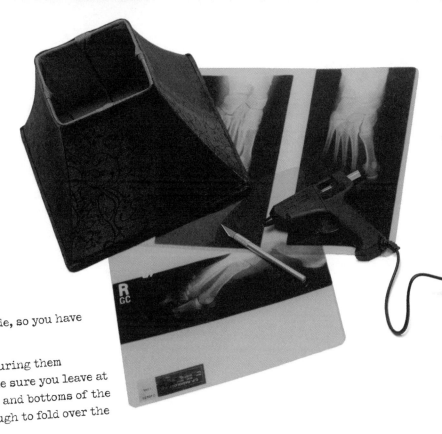

1. Remove the existing shade, so you have just the wire frame.

2. Cut your panels by measuring them against your frame. Make sure you leave at least ¾ inch on the tops and bottoms of the panels, so you have enough to fold over the lamp-shade frame.

3. Staple each of the panels onto the frame, top and bottom.

4. Finish off the edges with your tape.

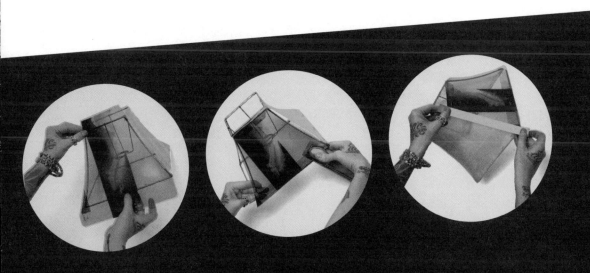

CHEAP-TO-CHIC COASTERS

It's simplest to use existing coasters, the ones you get at a bar.

YOU'LL ALSO NEED:

- Modge Podge
- Fabric scraps
- Scissors
- Small foam brush

1. Trim your fabric slightly larger than the coaster.

2. Brush a liberal coat of Modge Podge (MP) on the coaster, place the fabric over the top, and let it dry.

3. Using scissors, make small cuts in the excess fabric so it neatly folds over the edges of the coaster. Affix it with MP to the bottom.

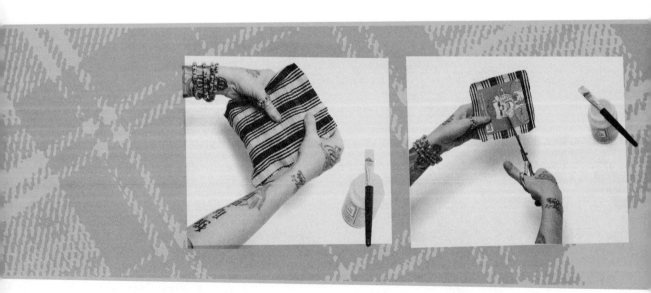

TIP: This same technique can be used for LOADS of other things; check out the guitar pick guard I covered in the same material for this custom First Act guitar!

4. Using a liberal coat of MP and your brush, coat the top of the fabric, fold the edges over, and let dry.

5. Use a smaller piece of fabric to finish the back. Adhere it following the instructions above. When it is set and dry, coat the entire piece once more with MP.

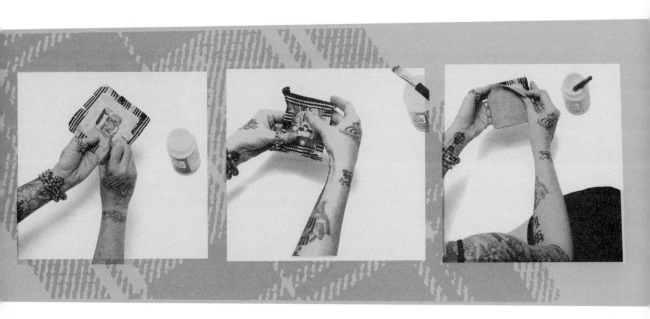

GAME TIME

Checkers!

WHAT YOU'LL NEED:

- 1 game board
- 16 metal bottle caps
- Resin (1 tube should be enough; about $6 at a hardware store)
- 2 sets of fun art* (e.g. nautical stars and hearts; 8 pieces each)
- Scissors

* I printed art out from my computer onto regular white paper.

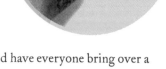

1. Take your art and cut it down to small 1-inch circles to fit inside the bottle caps.

2. Pour resin into the tops to set the art. Resin can take about 6 hours to set.

Once they're set, call up your friends and have everyone bring over a game and munchies for a cheap, "recession can't steal my fun" night in!

TIP: If you get some resin on the counter or on your fingers, you can use white vinegar to get it off!

MIRROR MIRROR

HAVE A MIRROR THAT'S BROKEN? Don't throw it away; you can turn it into a fun piece of art. Obviously, this is a project where you need to be **VERY** careful!

YOU'LL NEED:

- A mirror

- An old towel

- A hammer

- Epoxy (or strong glue)

- A piece of matte board (I used a piece of 8" x 10" black for this)

- Paints and foam brushes

- Glitter glue

- Rubber dishwashing gloves

- Thick silk ribbon (about 3 feet)

- Hot-glue gun

- 2 1" D rings (available at craft and fabric stores)

- 2 safety pins (any size)

continued...

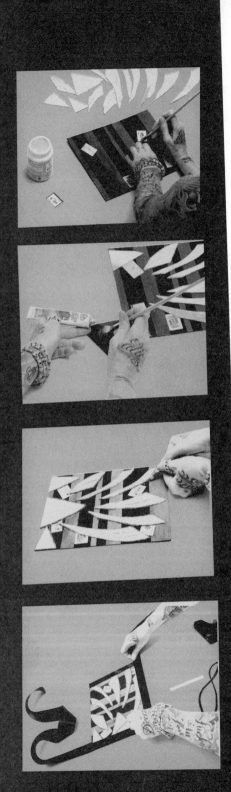

1. Start off by painting the matte board; you can do a solid color or a fun simple pattern, like stripes. (You can embellish—I added small paper playing cards I won at Coney Island to mine, affixing them with Modge Podge.)

2. If you don't have a broken mirror, then you can lay a perfectly good one between folds in a towel. VERY carefully, hit in the center with the hammer; this will give you some large shattered pieces.

3. Put on your rubber gloves and carefully pull out one of the large pieces, put glue on the back, and adhere it to the painted canvas.

4. Continue to piece the mirror back together like a puzzle on the canvas, leaving spaces in between so the design below shows through.

5. Use your glitter glue to trace the glass shard edges. I suggest throwing away the towel with smaller shards!

6. When the glue sets, grab your ribbon. It will become the frame and hanger.

7. Hot-glue your ribbon onto 3 of the edges; make sure to do front and back.

8. Use the remaining ribbon to hang your piece. You can knot the two ends together to suspend it. I got a little more creative and affixed 2 1" D rings with safety pins.

Cooler than anything you'll find in *Alice in Wonderland!*

CREATIVE WAYS TO STORE JEWELRY

Mannequin arms can be found for less than $30 on eBay. They don't need to be fancy—you'll be painting them anyway! Have fun with them: Paint them to match your space; paint on fun tattoo designs. Mount them on a base or save counter space and mount them on a wall.

T-SHIRTS AREN'T JUST CLOTHING!

Fashion to function, make some comfortable throw pillows with older tees.

WHAT YOU'LL NEED:

- Scissors
- Some scrap fabric
- Pillow stuffing (or cotton balls if you are lazy)
- Sewing machine
- Band tee
- Straight pins
- Needle and thread

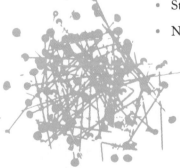

1. Cut out a large square from the front of the shirt, depending on how big you want your pillow to be. I suggest at least a 12-inch square; you'll lose about $\frac{1}{2}$ inch all the way around when you sew!

2. Cut a piece of fun scrap fabric the same size.

3. Straight-pin the edges of the tee and fabric "face to face."

4. Sew 3 of the sides totally, about $\frac{1}{4}$ inch in from the edges, and the 4th side about $\frac{3}{4}$ of the way across.

5. Turn the case right-side-out and stuff with the pillow stuffing. (If you're too lazy to go to the craft store, I suggest a lot of cotton balls from the 99-cent store.)

6. Use a needle and thread to hand-stitch the pillow shut.

ROCKIN' RECIPES

RAMEN NOODLES ARE HELL. They are like cardboard in water with chunks of confetti that are *supposed* to be veggies. When I was sixteen, at a friend's place, as usual it was all we had to eat. Nick tried to convince me he was a gourmet chef and that the trick to making them better was to use 50 percent water 50 percent beer and flavor them with cinnamon. I honestly don't remember the outcome (who knows; maybe I blocked it for a reason), but the point is, that's how I learned to cook. I've never had a formal lesson. Today in my fridge you are more apt to find strange condiments from my travels: dried ume from Japan, Jamaican rum runner sauce from Germany, instant white sauce mix from the U.K. . . . you get the idea. My own recipes usually have evolved from sheer trial and error. On the following pages, you'll see how instant pancake mix and tomatoes DO go together.

I decided to reach out to my friends and ask them for their vegetarian recipes. Some of my friends told funny stories, and some have nontraditional means of measuring and explaining things, which make these all the more fun. Why only veggie recipes? Well, I'm personally veggie and, honestly, at the end of the day, veggies are cheaper than meat when you're on a budget.

So enjoy the next few pages. Some recipes are superhealthy and require a stove; some are perfect for late-night munchies.

IN THE MORNING ...

BIFFY'S FAMOUS BREAKFAST FROM GOD

Bif Naked

WHEN I WAS IN MY EARLY 20S, I got turned on to Biffy's music. I was in love with it. I was floored by Bif—here was a girl, covered in ink, who was a brilliant musician, loved animals, was totally spiritual, and punk as fuck. I had an inkling of a feeling that at some point, sooner or later, our paths would cross. About six years ago they did, at a show she was doing in NYC. My friend Pete and I hit the show and (as Pete calls it) got "rockignized" by her publicist, Rikki Z. We didn't meet that night, but Rikki gave Bif a bunch of clothing I'd brought for her from my line, and the next time she was in town we got together. We did a shoot for *Inked Magazine* together, where we went to a Bad Brains reunion show at CBGB, and we've cooked together at Jivamukti Yoga Center (you can see the video at youtube.com/frankyandminx). This past year, Bif was diagnosed with breast cancer. I am still in total shock and can only say, this woman is amazing, and I pray her fighting spirit kicks her cancer's ass to the curb.

continued...

minx and Biffy

IN A VITA-MIX OR POWERFUL BLENDER:

- 3 big bananas
- 1 big handful spinach leaves
- 1 handful black kale leaves
- ¹/₂ pint blueberries
- 5 big strawberries
- 1 cup water

Blend until smooth.

IN A SHAKER CUP:

- 2 tbs flax meal
- 2 tbs shelled hempseeds
- 2 tbs whole psyllium husks

Combine with liquid and shake.

TIP: I always save half in a jar and put it in the fridge for an hour, which will solidify somewhat, due to the psyllium, and create a "pudding" for my midmorning snack! **Yummmmmmmm!**

Serves 1-2

ON-THE-LAM FRIED GREEN TOMATOES

ms minx

IN THE SUMMER, look for firm, medium-sized green tomatoes.
Farmer's markets are more likely to have them than grocery stores.

INGREDIENTS:

- 2 or 3 firm green tomatoes

- 1 egg (or Egg Beaters)

- Salt and pepper, to taste

- 1 cup Hungry Jack instant pancake mix

- 2 tbs Olivio, margarine, or butter

1. Cut tomatoes into thick slices, just less than ½ inch.

2. Then dip in egg or Egg Beaters, lightly coating both sides.

3. As usual, I was out of the basics, which is how I decided to improvise with Hungry Jack instant pancake mix. I added a few dashes of salt and pepper and fully coated the tomato slices in that instead of flour and cornmeal.

4. Next, heat a crepe pan superhot with Olivio (olive oil spread instead of butter) and cook them for about 2 minutes on each side.

YUM!!!

Serves 2 (unless you love them as much as I do and don't share)!

EASY HASH BROWNS

ms minx

IN '91 IN THE U.K., after going out on the road with International Beat, the band got in late to a friend's house. We didn't have the energy to go to the food store, so we were left with what was in the fridge (not much!). There were some potatoes, onions, and eggs. The band had been talking about how they loved American breakfast food, so I went to town.

INGREDIENTS:

- Potatoes (2-3 fist-sized)
- ½ onion
- 1 egg white
- Oil

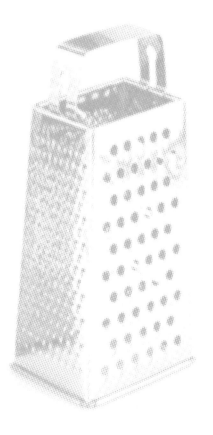

1. Use a cheese grater to shred up the potatoes (no need to peel them, skins are fine!). Once you grate them into a bowl, there will be some extra liquid; just blot it off with a paper towel.

2. Dice up the onion and mix it in with the grated potato (to taste).

3. Use 1 egg white for every cup and a half of the potato-and-onion mixture; stir it all up well.

4. Heat up a skillet and put in some oil. Make small patties out of the potato and lay in the pan. Put the lid on and let them cook well—at least 8 minutes on a medium heat—flipping them several times. They should be crispy on both sides.

Serves 2

EGGLESS FRENCH TOAST

Porcell of YOUTH OF TODAY/JUDGE

PORCELL AND I met backstage at the BNB Bowl '09, albeit for a super-short time. He wound up reading an interview I had done for my nonprofit, and reached out to me. It was funny, but when I asked him for a recipe, the first one he gave me was for Khichari — which **was** funny, because John Joseph had already given me that one. What are the odds of that? Porcell and I share a love of India, but here is a totally American breakfast for you.

INGREDIENTS:

- 6 slices of bread (soft whole-wheat or multigrain is ideal)
- 3 tablespoons tahini
- 1 cup milk or soy milk
- 1 ripe banana, mashed well
- 1 tablespoon maple syrup
- 1/2 teaspoon vanilla
- 1 teaspoon cinnamon
- 3 tablespoons whole-wheat pastry flour
- 2 tablespoons butter (or olive oil)

1. Set aside the bread and combine all the other ingredients except the butter in a large mixing bowl, adding the flour last.

2. Preheat griddle or frying pan on a high heat, melting butter on the surface so the bread doesn't stick (olive oil can be substituted for vegan French toast). If you use butter, make sure you get the bread onto the griddle quickly or the butter may burn. Ghee (clarified butter, available at Indian markets or health food stores) can also be used and has a much higher burn temperature than butter. If your pan has a nonstick surface, you can forgo the butter or oil altogether, but make sure the pan has a chance to get nice and hot.

3. Coat the bread well with the mixture and after shaking off the excess batter, place on griddle. After about 30 seconds, reduce flame to a medium heat and flip when the bottom becomes golden brown (may take another minute or two, depending on the stove). Turn flame back to high and repeat the process for the other side.

4. Serve hot topped with extra butter (or vegan substitute) and pure maple syrup, with fresh fruit of your choice on the side.

Serves 2-3

EGG SANDWICH

Lou Koller of SICK OF IT ALL

LOU AND I HAVE KNOWN EACH OTHER for about ten years. I've been on the road with his band, and over the years they have supported me in many ways. I had to reach out to him last minute for this and, as always, he came through!

INGREDIENTS:

- 3 eggs
- ¼ cup milk
- Garlic powder, to taste
- Salt and pepper, to taste
- 2 slices of whole-wheat bread
- 2 slices of cheese (whatever kind you like; I use good old American!)

1. Grease up your frying pan and put it on the fire!

2. Break the eggs into a bowl and add milk.

3. Put in the garlic powder; how much depends on you. I do it by eye, so wing it. Add the salt and pepper to flavor.

4. Now beat the whole thing 'til your wrist and elbow ache! Pour it all into the hot pan.

5. Put the whole-wheat bread into the toaster now, 'cause the eggs cook fast.

6. Keep running a spatula around the edge and keep scrambling the eggs 'til they're done to your liking. Put the cheese on the toast and then put the eggs on top of the cheese and squish it all together.

Serves 1

SOUPS...

DIRTYROTTENLOVE'S HEARTY UKRAINIAN BORSCHT

dirtyrottenlove (aka Helen)

DIRTYROTTENLOVE (aka Helen on the PRD boards) may not be in a band, but I don't care—'cuz she rocks! Somehow, Helen volunteered to help moderate the boards, which is no small task. I'm still trying to figure out how she has time to cook such yummy veggie goodness!

"OK ... this recipe is really versatile because you can make as much or as little as you want depending on how hearty of a soup you prefer. I really like loads of veggies in my soup, but feel free to play around with the ingredients."

INGREDIENTS:

- 6–7 medium-sized beets
- ¹/₂ cup shredded carrot
- ¹/₂ cup chopped onion
- ¹/₂ cup celery
- 1–2 bay leaves
- Extra virgin olive oil
- Salt and pepper, to taste
- Pepper
- ¹/₂ tsp chopped garlic (I use the kind from the jar)
- 1 red bell pepper, diced
- 1 green bell pepper, diced
- 1 bunch *fresh* dill, chopped extremely fine
- 1 can crushed tomatoes
- 1 medium-sized potato, cubed
- ¹/₂ cup fresh shredded cabbage, if desired
- 1 can kidney beans
- Sour salt

1. Wash beets thoroughly. Cut the stems off and throw away. Place the beets (still with skins on) in a large stockpot and fill pot with water. Cook beets until they are tender when pierced with a fork.

2. While the beets are cooking, sauté the carrots, onion, celery, and bay leaves in the olive oil. Add salt and pepper. Once they are almost cooked, add in the chopped garlic and chopped bell peppers. Once this is complete, set aside.

3. When beets are cooked, remove from stock. Filter the broth/stock through a cheesecloth. Since beets are a root vegetable, it is best to drain the broth as best as possible to eliminate anything that broke away from the beets during boiling.

4. Gently peel the skin from the beets with your fingers and grate the beets into long julienne-like strips.

5. Pour the entire contents of your sautéed veggies into the broth (oil and all!). Add the finely chopped dill, tomato, potato, cabbage, and entire can of beans (undrained). Simmer.

6. The soup is about done when the potatoes are tender when pierced with a fork, so be sure not to cut them too little or you will have mashed potatoes in your soup!

7. Once the soup is complete, add a small pinch of sour salt and stir. Taste the soup; it should have a little sour kick to it . . . if it doesn't, add another SMALL pinch of the sour salt. Keep doing this until you reach the desired taste, but be careful with sour salt because if you add a pinch too much, it will ruin the soup.

8. Remove and enjoy! You can add a dollop of sour cream if desired, but I prefer it plain! And borscht is best reheated the next day!

Makes about 2 quarts

MINX'S NOTE: When I made this I nixed the peppers and used diced apples instead. I also replaced the potato with sweet potato and added a dash of English ale to the beets when they were boiling.

BEAN SOUP À LA LEELEE

Freddy Cricien of MADBALL

LIKE BROTHER, LIKE BROTHER. Freddy, like his half brother Roger Miret, texted this to me from the road. In addition to singing for NYHC mainstay Madball, Freddy also runs Black N Blue Productions with Cuz Joe—which I have helped with since day one, I am proud to say.

Courtesy of Jeff Pliskin, Raised First Propaganda

INGREDIENTS:

- 1 large yellow onion
- 1 to 1 ½ tbs chopped garlic
- 1 package greens or kale
- 2 cans white northern beans
- 1 can adzuki beans
- 1 can butter beans
- 2 cartons vegetable broth
- Salt and pepper, to taste

1. Sauté the onions and garlic in a large pot in a little extra virgin olive oil.

2. After a few minutes add about a cup of vegetable broth. When the broth starts to boil, slowly add the greens until they soften a bit.

3. Drain the beans and add them to the pot. Add the rest of the vegetable broth. Bring it to a boil, then simmer for about 30 minutes. (Don't forget to season with salt and pepper throughout the cooking process.) Voilà!

Makes about 2 quarts

CUBAN BLACK BEAN SOUP

Roger Miret of AGNOSTIC FRONT, THE DISASTERS

I GREW UP LISTENING TO AGNOSTIC FRONT—listening to their music on mix tapes. I still have one and can't believe it's not worn thin and distorted from how much my friends and I would play it on our drives to D.C. for shows at the old 9:30 Club. After moving to NYC, Roger and I became friendly. I've always had a massive respect for how he continues to push ahead—the Disasters, endless touring, and his Dirty Devil Apparel line. Roger texted me this recipe back in 2005 when PRD first started, from the van, on the road on tour.

INGREDIENTS:

- Olive oil

- 2 small cloves chopped garlic

- 1 small onion, diced

- 1 small green pepper, diced

- 1 small tomato, diced

- 2 packages Sazón Goya
  (con Safrin, makes it a yellowy red tint)

- Cilantro!

- 1 can Goya Black Beans, unseasoned

continued...

minx and Roger Miret at CBGBs

Courtesy of Viva Van Story, vivaspinups.com

1. In a small pot bring olive oil to medium heat, add garlic lightly brown; add onions, peppers, and Sazón packages.

2. Add beans (make sure they have been washed out of the water they were in in the can).

3. Add some water (not too much . . . don't want it too soupy!) add cilantro and put flame low so everything can cook slowly and absorb the flavors.

4. Add tomatoes . . . cook another 5 minutes . . .

5. And eat with rice!   Make sure you use Canilla rice! Or Goya! Wash the rice to get the starch out!

6. For each cup of rice add 2 cups of water . . . bring to a boil. Add touch of salt and tsp of olive oil, mix and bring it to cook low till fluffy and done! If you want to make the rice yellow add a package of the Sazón Goya (con Safrin) in the water as it is boiling!

Makes about 1 quart

SNACKS ...

CLAY'S FAMOUS CRYING LATER SALSA

Clay of LOWER CLASS BRATS, THE F-BOMBERS

CLAY AND I MET through his supertalented girlfriend, Kimpulsive. We were working on a clothing-line project together that entailed twenty-four-hours' straight work in their garage in Jersey, covered in paint. All I can say is, if you want to get to know someone, spend twenty-four hours straight with them, awake and exhausted. Clay can make jokes quicker than anyone I know and uses the word "buddy" like I use the word "thingie."

"I've been making this sauce since I was nineteen. It started off as an experiment, but I ended up keeping it. Goes good on EVERYTHING except ice cream. I call it Crying Later Salsa. You should find out why!"

INGREDIENTS:

- 5 fresh tomatoes

- ½ red onion

- 6 fresh jalapeño peppers

- 12 dried chipotle peppers* (at least)

- 3 fresh serrano peppers

- 1 tbs minced garlic

- 1 tbs salt

- 1 tbs garlic powder (optional)

* Make sure to crush chipotle peppers by hand with a mortar — just make sure they get chopped up as fine as possible. Grindin' them up beforehand is definitely recommended. If not, they are hard, so they can make your processor start dancin' all over the counter and spittin' vegetable goo all over the place.

1. Put all the ingredients into the processor and hit the button. The consistency should be "kinda runny," but you can blend it to your desired consistency—just blend the shit out of it.

2. After it sits for 24 hours and the ingredients get more comfortable being around each other, it really gets a killer smoky flavor. It always gets better the 2nd day, so if you're gonna bring it somewhere, always prepare it a day ahead of time. Oh, and keep it in your fridge. It makes **a lot.**

Makes about 4-5 cups

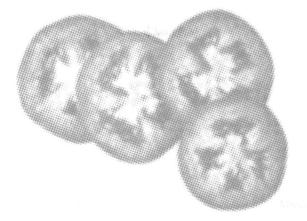

Kimpulsive and Clay have a great way of packaging the F-Bombers CDs. They silk-screen canvas, so that people can cut them apart and have a band patch!

Lu supporting Franky & Minx
late night in a deli, after a gig

CON QUESO DIP

Lu of SUB ZERO

"OK, here is a quick appetizer recipe that is easy to make and great for parties!!"

INGREDIENTS:

- 1 package (8 oz) cream cheese
- 8 oz Colby Jack cheese
  (grated or cut into small cubes)
- 1 can Hormel Vegetarian Chili
  (*You can make your own chili,* ~~but why?~~)

1. Put it all in a big bowl.

2. Microwave it 'til it all melts (1–3 minutes; microwaves differ, just keep your eye on it).

3. Remove and mix it all together.

4. Throw a big dollop of sour cream on it.

"IT'S ~~FRICKIN~~ DELICIOUS!!!!"

Makes about 4 cups

MINX'S INDIAN TACO

ms minx

AS I WAS PREPARING to head back to India this past summer for my work with Built on Respect, I decided to use the downtime to find new ways to make snacks with Indian ingredients. This is a prevailing favorite.

INGREDIENTS:

- 1 piece nan bread or roti
- 3–4 cloves of roasted garlic
- $1/2$ small tomato
- Plain yogurt (known as curd in Indian stores)
- Coriander chutney
- Salt and pepper, to taste

1. Toast the bread of your choice.
2. Schmear on your roasted garlic cloves.
3. Dice 'n slice your tomato; pile it on top.
4. Add about 3 tsp of plain yogurt and 2 tsp of the coriander chutney.
5. Sprinkle on a 'lil salt 'n pepper, fold it up, and enjoy!

Serves 1

Courtesy of Christopher Donaz

NATE'S WORLD-FAMOUS GUACAMOLE

Nathen Maxwell of FLOGGING MOLLY

INGREDIENTS:

- 3 large ripe avocados (preferably Hass)
- ½ large white or red onion (or 1 small), finely chopped
- ½ bunch cilantro (coriander), finely chopped
- 1 jalapeño, de-seeded and diced (leaving seeds in will make the guacamole a lot spicier)
- Juice of ½ lime
- Salt to taste (about 1 tsp)
- 1 medium tomato, chopped

1. Cut the avocados in half around the seed from top to bottom. Slightly twist the two sides to open. To remove seed, carefully hit it with sharp side of knife so that knife sticks into the seed, then twist the seed out with the knife. Using a spoon, scoop out inside of avocado into a large mixing bowl.

2. Add onion, cilantro, jalapeño, lime juice, and salt.

3. Mash all together using a masher, spoon, or whatever until pretty smooth.

4. Gently stir in tomato.

   Serve with your favorite corn tortilla chips.
   Enjoy! Vegan, healthy, and delicious!

"Talk about a total food stoke when showing up at your friend's BBQ with Nate's World-Famous Guacamole! Guaranteed to be invited back! (Unless, of course, if you drink too many of Nate's World-Famous Margaritas, and, well, you can imagine . . .)"

Yields 1 batch

HUMMUS VEGGIE PIZZA

Elvis Cortez of LEFT ALONE

IN HIS OWN WORDS, "How many punk rock Mexicans do you know with pink Mohawks?" Elvis has always been one of the most DIY people I know. He's down to earth and funny as hell. I couldn't resist asking him to contribute!

INGREDIENTS:

- Hummus
- 1 whole wheat pita, 7"-round
- Lettuce
- 1 cucumber

1. Spread a fat portion of hummus on top of your pita.

2. Add some lettuce.

3. Cut thin slices of cucumber and 'yer done.

"You can also just fold it in half—and, BAM, hummus taco. I eat this all the time on tour; it's the best."

Serves 1

Elvis backstage at *Dead American Radio* release show

All images courtesy of CH3

BAKED ONIONS

Kimm Gardner of CHANNEL THREE

I love to eat! If I did not work too many hours in a crazy job (that I love), play in a band, have kids and a wife, I would want to run a restaurant and bar . . . think of Cheers for my neighborhood in Long Beach, California.

Recipes used to be something only women talked about, but many of the "dude" friends of mine are great cooks and can toss together great meals, and they are not just things done on a BBQ!

The recipe that I want to suggest is from my family, and sounds very White Trashy, but try it once and you will be hooked. This recipe goes great with anything. Try it on top of a warm sandwich, and you will not be sorry.

This is something that people ask me to bring to Thanksgiving, a BBQ, or any dinner setting.

INGREDIENTS:

- 30 saltine crackers, crushed
- 3/4 cup melted butter
- 3 cups thinly sliced onions
- 1/2 lb grated cheddar cheese
- 1 1/2 cups milk
- 3 eggs
- 1/2 tsp salt and pepper

1. Mix saltines and $\frac{1}{2}$ cup of melted butter together and place in the bottom of a 9" x 9" pan.

2. Sauté thinly sliced onions in $\frac{1}{4}$ cup of butter until transparent. Spread on top of cracker mixture.

3. Spread grated cheddar cheese on top of onions.

4. Scald milk on stove, remove from heat, and whisk in well-beaten eggs. Stir in salt and pepper. Pour over onion/cheese mixture.

5. Bake at 350° F. for $\frac{1}{4}$ hour and serve. Enjoy!

Serves 4-5

THEO'S VEGAN RANCH DIP

Courtesy of Theo Kogan

Theo of LUNACHICKS, THEO & THE SKYSCRAPERS

THEO AND I MET through friends several years ago. Whenever we can, we make it a point to get good veggie food together. Theo's brilliant. Besides fronting the Lunachicks and Theo & the Skyscrapers, she's started her own animal-product-free lip-gloss line called Armour Beauty. It's yummy, and so are her recipes!

INGREDIENTS:

- Juice of 1/2 lemon
- 1/2 cup Vegenaise
- 2 tbs nutritional yeast
- 1 tsp French mustard
- 1 tsp hot sauce (such as Trappey's Red Devil)
- 1 pinch sugar
- Cracked pepper, to taste
- 1/2 tsp water (if needed)

Add all ingredients into a small mixing bowl and mix by hand 'til all are combined.

Serves 4

SERVING SUGGESTIONS

As a dip: for veggie chicken nuggets, celery sticks and carrot sticks, and faux chicken or faux fish finger foods. **OR as a spread:** for sandwiches and wraps.

REAL MEALS...

AMES' NEW YEAR'S DAY
(Black-Eyed Peas, Collard Greens, and Hot-Water Corn Bread)

Amy Fields

FOR NEW YEAR'S DAY 2008, I hightailed it over to Ames and Noah's place. Ames is one of my dearest friends from New York, and after she moved to L.A., she married Noah from Dharma Punx. We had the most chill New Year's Day, with Ames cooking a traditional Texas New Year's Day feast: black-eyed peas, collard greens, and hot-water corn bread.

According to Ames:

"The peas and greens are a Southern New Year's Day tradition. They signify health, wealth, and prosperity—don't ask me which is which, though. I have no idea! You're just supposed to eat them to bring luck to the new year . . . but they just taste good, too!"

INGREDIENTS:

- 4 carrots, chopped
- 4 celery stalks, cut into small pieces
- 2 small yellow onions
- Canola oil
- Salt and pepper, to taste
- Tumeric
- Cayenne
- Thyme
- Bay leaf
- 1 cup veggie stock

- 2 cups black-eyed peas, rinsed and soaked
- Red pepper flakes
- 2 cloves minced garlic
- 2 lbs collard greens, chopped into 3" strips
- 1 pat of butter
- ¼ cup apple cider or red wine vinegar (optional)
- 2 cups cornmeal
- 3 green onions, chopped
- Fresh tomatoes

continued...

minx and Ames in a random NY photo booth!

Black-Eyed Peas

1. Sauté carrots, celery, and yellow onion in about 2 tsp of canola oil. Throw in salt and pepper, some thyme (fresh or dry), and a bay leaf. Deglaze with a little veggie stock.

2. Add the remaining veggie stock and/or water. I usually do a combo. How much depends on how soupy you like your peas. Add your peas and bring to a boil, then turn down to a simmer and cook for a few hours or until tender.

Collard Greens

1. Heat some olive oil and red pepper flakes in a large skillet.

2. Put in some sliced garlic (I like a lot), then add your washed and chopped collard greens.

3. Sauté for a while and add a splash or two of veggie stock, cover and let the greens steam a few minutes, then finish with a pat of butter. I like to add a splash of apple cider or red wine vinegar, but Noah the Yankee–Santa Cruz does not.

Hot-Water Corn Bread

1. Put cornmeal in a bowl. Add plenty of salt. And I like a bit of turmeric and cayenne pepper.

2. Mix the dry ingredients, then add enough boiling water so the consistency is kinda like wet sand. Stir in green onions.

3. Meanwhile, heat up about a ½ inch of canola oil over medium heat in a cast-iron skillet if you have it (but not necessary, a regular one is fine). You know the oil's hot enough when you flick some water off your fingers and it sizzles.

4. Drop in large spoon-size patties of the corn-bread mixture and pan-fry on both sides until they get a slight golden brown; drain on a paper towel. Serve with a pat of butter on top and eat in your greens or dunk in your peas.

Serve all this with a side of homegrown tomatoes (that means heirloom for most of us) and you've got a perfectly vegetarian New Year's Day lunch. You won't even miss the bacon grease and salt pork!!!

Serves 4

THE HILTZ FAMILY BBQ TOFU

Kate Hiltz of THE BOUNCING SOULS

"Kate's great. The evidence of this can be found in her cooking! I feel blessed to have her in my life. I don't know where I, or any of the Souls, would be without her."
— Bryan Kienlan

KATE'S AN INSEPARABLE PART of The Bouncing Souls and Chunksaah Records family. In fact, in 2009, she spearheaded the Souls' completely DIY release of their album *The 20th Anniversary Collection*, which saw one track per month being released digitally by the band themselves!

This is the recipe that I make the most ... it's everyone's favorite for sure. My brother actually gave me the recipe (he was famous for serving it at his house shows in the '90s) and I tweaked it a bit so that now we argue incessantly about whose is better! It doesn't matter how much you make, it always goes ... frequently gets finished with forks right out of the pan after the show when everyone is tipsy and starving! You know I'm not so great at measuring, but here's the gist of it. —Kate Hiltz

INGREDIENTS:

- 3 packages extra-firm tofu
- 1 cup creamy peanut butter
- 2 teaspoons tahini
- 1 cup canola oil
- Salt and pepper, to taste

- Garlic powder

- Paprika

- 1 tbs sesame seeds

- 2–3 bottles BBQ sauce of your choice

1. Freeze packages of extra-firm tofu overnight and then defrost. Open the packages and squeeze all of the water out of them. (The freezing process changes the texture of the tofu so it's way more spongy . . . and less breakable!)

2. In a big bowl, mix together the creamy peanut butter, tahini, and canola oil. Add salt, pepper, garlic powder, and paprika to taste.

3. Cut the tofu into 8 pieces per block (so they are like 2" x 3" x $\frac{1}{2}$") and coat them all in the peanut butter mixture. Let it all soak in and stir occasionally for even coatage.

4. Preheat oven to 375° F, spread tofu on a baking sheet, and bake for about 45 minutes, flipping 2-3 times.

5. Then put a bunch of sesame seeds all over them, raise temperature to 425° F, and bake for another 10-15 minutes.

6. Get 2–3 bottles of yummy BBQ sauce (I like Annie's Smokey Maple, but there are so many to love) and pour them all over that shit, cooking another 5 minutes and stirring it all to make it sesame-BBQ-PB glommy goodness!

Serves 5

VEGETABLES, LENTILS, CASHEWS, AND BASMATI RICE (KHICHARI)

John Joseph of BLOODCLOT, CRO-MAGS

A LONG TIME AGO, I was in the East Village hangout, Manitoba's (of Handsome Dick Manitoba/Dictators' fame), and met John. John and I live in the same neighborhood, so we're forever walking into each other. John has been Krishna for years; he cooks amazing veggie feasts each week for the downtown homeless, and has also written his own books, *Evolution of a Cro-Magnon* and *Meat is for Pussies*. John is hands-down one of the best people I know and an AMAZING inspiration. His recipe is good for you and your spirit.

This is a nutritious stew that is high in protein. I strongly recommend using organic veggies, rice, and beans, and nonirradiated spices.

This recipe is mildly spiced.

INGREDIENTS (CHECK YOUR LOCAL ORGANIC GROCER):

- 3 tbs ghee or oil
- 2 tsp cumin seeds
- 1 tbs fresh hot green chili, minced
- 2 tbs minced fresh ginger
- 1 tsp turmeric
- 1 tsp yellow asafetida powder
- 3 cups mixed vegetables (broccoli, cauliflower, zucchini), cut into large chunks
- 1 cup split red lentils
- 1 cup basmati or other long-grain white rice
- 5–6 cups water

- 1½ tsp salt

- 1 tbs organic butter or soy margarine (no trans fat)

- 1 cup seitan, stir-fried in sesame oil for 5 minutes

- 1 cup cooked green peas

- 1 cup tomatoes, peeled and chopped

- 2 cups fresh spinach, chopped

- cup cooked unsalted cashews

- ½ cup fresh coriander leaves, chopped

minx with John and Craig at Black N Blue Bowl '08

1. Heat the ghee in a heavy 4-liter, nonstick saucepan over moderate heat. Sprinkle the cumin seeds into the ghee. When they turn golden brown, add the chilies and ginger. Sauté them for a few seconds, then add the turmeric and asafetida. Add the vegetable pieces and fry them for a minute or two.

2. Stir in the lentils and rice, mixing with the spices and vegetables for a minute.

3. Pour in the water and bring to a full boil over high heat. Reduce the heat to low, partially cover, and slowly cook, stirring occasionally, for about 30 minutes or until the lentils and rice are soft. If the khichari dries out too much, add up to 1 cup warm water.

4. Fold in the salt, butter, seitan, cooked green peas, chopped tomatoes, spinach, toasted cashews, and chopped fresh coriander leaves, allowing them to warm for 5 minutes. Serve hot with fresh organic bread.

Serves 6-8

SUNDAY DECEMBER 28
ROCKS OFF PRESENTS

Cro-Mags

FEATURING
JOHN JOSEPH * MACKIE
AJ/LEEWAY * CRAIG/SICK OF IT ALL
PLUS SPECIAL GUESTS
WISDOM IN CHAINS
TRAPPED UNDER ICE
PLUS MORE TBA!

$15 @ THE KNITTING FACTORY
DOORS 5:30 / SHOW 6:00

A % OF THE PROCEEDS GO TO:
BUILT on RESPECT

VEGGIE PHILLY CHEESESTEAK

Johnny Rioux of STREET DOGS

When street dogs go on tour, Philadelphia is always in our top 3 or 4 cities to play. The shows go off, the kids are great, and the city is top-notch! We always find our way to South Street at some point, and our first stop is always Gianna's, just off South on 6th St. Evidently it is also the stop for many bands, because there are band posters and testimonials all over the walls there.

I am a vegetarian, but my bandmates are not. However, when it comes to cheesesteaks done Philly-style, there is something for everyone at Gianna's. I swear you cannot tell the difference from the veggie steaks. Word of caution, however: With so much soy product, make sure you are close to a restroom for a good 24 hours! When I come home for a good amount of time (a rarity), I find myself craving that Philly cheesesteak. So here is the recipe for those desperate times . . .

WHAT YOU'LL NEED:

Tools:

- Large saucepan
- Wooden spoon
- Tongs

Ingredients:

- 1 tbs oil
- Medium yellow onion, thinly sliced

Courtesy of Kirsten DeBoer

- Mushrooms, if you like them

- Medium bell pepper, seeded and cut into strips

- $^1/_2$ lb seitan, thinly sliced (It is difficult to find proper seitan in many grocery stores, so a good plan B is MorningStar Farms Veggie Steak Strips. Just defrost and cut even thinner than it comes.)

- 1 tbs vegetarian Worcestershire sauce

- 1 tbs Guinness (not sure why—but it sounds good and adds a bit of flavor)

- Salt and pepper, to taste

- Italian seasoning to taste, but not too much containing salt (seitan can be really salty).

- 4 oz mozzarella cheese, shredded, or bottle of Cheez Whiz

- 2 sub rolls, pieces of French or Italian bread, or Kaiser rolls

1. Heat oil over medium heat, then stir in onion, mushrooms, and bell pepper. Cover and sauté, stirring occasionally, about 5 minutes, until soft.

2. Add seitan, cook for 2–3 minutes until golden, turn, and repeat. Stir in Worcestershire, Guinness, salt and pepper, then top with cheese and let sit until it melts.

3. Assemble the sandwiches and serve!

Serves 2 **hungry** punk rockers.

Courtesy of Helena Bxl

PASTA À LA SARSA

Chris Michez of DO OR DIE

FOR CHRISTMAS DAY 2008, I got together with friends, Laurens and Helena from I Scream Records, Emma, and Chris, who is in the Belgian band Do or Die. Instead of cooking for ourselves, we decided to cook for the many people who spend their days in Tompkins Square Park in New York.

We kept it simple; we wanted to make a simple, warm meal for as many as possible in my very small kitchen. The recipe is below, and considering the number of smiles it generated that day, I can highly recommend it!

INGREDIENTS:

- Olive oil
- 4 garlic cloves
- 2 cans peeled tomatoes
- Salt and pepper, to taste
- 1 tbs sugar
- 4 diced basil leaves
- 250 grams pasta per person

1. Put olive oil in a pan and let it warm up. Add the garlic (cut in pieces) and let simmer. Add the peeled tomatoes and salt, pepper, and sugar. Add basil.

2. Put the pasta to a boil, serve al dente, and add sauce on top.

Serves 4

Clay of LOWER CLASS BRATS, THE F-BOMBERS

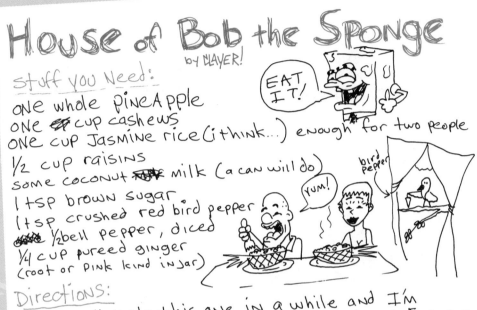

House of Bob the Sponge
by CLAYER!

Stuff you Need:

ONE whole PiNEApple
ONE ~~¾~~ cup cashews
ONE cup Jasmine rice (i think...) enough for two people
½ cup raisins
Some coconut ~~not~~ milk (a can will do)
1 tsp brown sugar
1 tsp crushed red bird pepper
~~~~ ½ bell pepper, diced
¼ cup pureed ginger
(root or PiNk kind in Jar)

EAT IT!

YUM!

bird pepper

Directions:

I haven't made this one in a while and I'm writing this from memory. it's a good one, I swear. Take your PiNEApple and cut iN half like so: take a SPOON and carefully scoop out the innards.* cut into cubes and place off to the side. Next, make the rice according to directions on package, except use ½ water and ½ coconut milk. once rice is done, combine all other ingredients including pineapple chunks. If you are a pepper sissy, go easy on the crushed red bird pepper. a little goes a long way. Stir it all together and fill pineapple halves. wrap in tinfoil and place in the oven on 325° for about 10 min. after 10 min, remove, unwrap and enjoy! add your own stuff to this one, email me any positive results.
asitissobeit@yahoo.com

* do Not toss out piNEApple shell! you will need it.

DA BOMB VEGGIE STIR-FRY

White Owl of WHITE OWL & THE GOTHAM CITY PLAYERS

WHITE OWL, AKA AARON, and I have known each other for years. He's one of those friends I can't remember meeting but can't remember ever not knowing. His smile is infectious and his recipe is da bomb.

minx and Aaron

INGREDIENTS:

- Olive oil
- Eggplant
- Tofu
- Green pepper
- Teriyaki sauce
- Fresh broccoli
- Tomato
- Onion
- Avocado

1. Here's the deal. Heat a little olive oil (enough to just layer the pan) at medium-low heat. A wok is ideal, but I don't have one, and a large pan does the job.

2. Slice up some eggplant (any way you like), and when the oil starts to get hot, throw that in first.

3. Wait 5 minutes, then throw in the sliced-up tofu and green pepper. At this point cover the whole thing with some teriyaki sauce (enough to cover everything) and mix it all up.

4. You want to steam the broccoli on the side while all this is going down. Just boil the broccoli in a pot with $\frac{1}{4}$ cup of water. When water boils, turn heat to medium-low, then cover to steam (about 5 minutes).

5. Broccoli should be drained and thrown in with cut-up tomato, onion, and avocado a couple of minutes after the tofu and pepper were thrown in!

6. Now comes the personal touch—the most important part—the spice. This is up to you, but I recommend some heavy shakes of salt, some dabs of pepper, some lemon pepper (that's my favorite), and some garlic powder. At this point you may want to throw in some more teriyaki sauce and mix it up for a couple more minutes and—VOILÀ—White Owl's Veggie Stir-fry.

CHILL OUT! PEACE!!

Serves 4

FAILED ECONOMIC POLICY SURPRISE SALAD

Bruce Wingate of ADRENALIN O.D.

INGREDIENTS:

- 1 can (16 oz) of red beans, drained
- 1 big or 2 small tomatoes
- ½ cucumber
- ½ red pepper
- Red onion
- Cilantro
- Rice vinegar

The beauty of this dish lies in its ability to adapt and evolve according to the ingredients at hand. Feel free to remix, for it is the way of the trickle-down salad.

ADRENALIN O.D.

N.Y.C POLICE
120 762
4 4 58

sentimental abuse

1. Drain and rinse beans. Cut tomatoes in half and scoop out the guts. Rinse and cut up vegetables. I like to chop everything to bits with a really big knife.

2. Mix ingredients in large salad bowl.

3. Season to taste and chill.

Failed Economic Policy Surprise Salad is a perfect unification of healthy eating and budgetary limitations. One can substitute a host of improvised ingredients, whether they are shoplifted or given to you while visiting Mom.

SUGGESTIONS: Feta or Gorgonzola cheese, chick peas, lemon, lime, or your favorite pasta (to stretch another meal out of it).

The late Randy "Biscuit" Turner of the seminal Texas skate-punk band The Big Boys used to encourage his audiences to "go form your own band." It is in this spirit I encourage you to "go form your own salad."

Serves 2 unemployed people

All images courtesy of AOD

SWEET T🕱TH...

DESSERT PIZZA

Noah Levine of DHARMA PUNX

INGREDIENTS:

- Trader Joe's pizza crust (we like the whole-wheat one)
- Ricotta cheese
- Mozzarella cheese
- Gorgonzola cheese
- Halved mission figs
- Honey (optional)

1. Start with the Trader Joe's pizza crust. Slather on ricotta, mozzarella, and Gorgonzola cheeses, then top with some halved mission figs—also found at Trader Joe's.

2. Then just bake according to instructions on the pizza crust.

So yummy!!!!!!!!!! You can also drizzle with honey when it comes out of the oven!!!!!

Serves 3-4

Courtesy of Shannon Brooke

Heidi...
I love you girl.
Thank you for everything!
Love,
Colleen xo

DEVIL DOLL'S FORBIDDEN FRUIT DESSERT

Colleen Duffy of DEVIL DOLL

I CAN'T THINK of a single time that listening to Devil Doll's music just hasn't made everything better. Whether DJing, lounging in bed, or romping around the streets of NYC, I LOVE her music and wit, and never tire of it. Colleen (the Devil Doll herself) shared some of that yummy sexiness and style with her signature dessert.

INGREDIENTS:

- 1 cup sifted flour, all-purpose or gluten-free

- 1 cup and 2 tbs sugar or xylitol

- 1 tsp baking powder

- 1/4 tsp salt

- 1 1/2–3 tbs of room-temperature butter

- 1 egg

- 1/2 tsp vanilla

- Milk or milk substitute

- 3–4 cups sliced fruit (pears, apples, peaches, plums . . .)

- 2 tsp cinnamon

1. Preheat oven to 425° F.

2. Sift all-purpose flour or gluten-free flour into a bowl. (Make sure you **SIFT THE FLOUR** . . . unless you like your baked goods to have secret explosive pockets of sand-tasting powder . . . mmmmmm.)

3. In a separate, smaller bowl, combine 2 tbs sugar or xylitol, baking powder, and salt. They are dry ingredients, so you can literally stir them together with your finger. It is important they are evenly mixed together before adding them to the flour, so that the person you are trying to seduce with this heavenly dessert does not feel like they

just chewed into a salt lick. (Unless you are into some kind of Bambi thing, which at that point, if it's consensual . . . hey, let your freak flag fly.)

4. Pour your small bowl of dry ingredients into your large bowl of flour and mix them together with a fork, spoon, knife, or some other implement borrowed from your secret "How-to-Off-an-Ex Toolbox." If this secret box of karma-ending cutlery is empty, I suggest you move before someone discovers the bodies in your backyard or, worse yet, some weird zombie thing happens because . . . well, they know where you live.

5. Add 1½–3 tbs of room-temperature butter and mix. (Adjust the amount of butter according to how juicy the fruit is. For example, pears are extremely juicy, so you want a smaller amount of butter as to not end up with "The Forbidden Soup.")

6. In a measuring cup, beat together 1 whole egg and ½ tsp of vanilla. Then add enough milk or milk substitute to make a ½ cup mixture. Pour this mixture into your bowl and combine together to make a stiff dough. Feel free to use your hands. After satisfied, pat the dough into your 9" x 9" Pyrex or pan. You are now going to take 3–4 cups of your favorite sliced, sexy fruit and begin laying them in overlapping rows across your crust. The most sinfully delicious combination I have found is to use the sweetest apples mixed with Bartlett pears. This is a heavy water content, so watch the butter. You can also use peaches, plums, etc. Don't be afraid to get creative; the nuns can't hurt you anymore.

7. You are going to sprinkle the top of this seductive, "get-into-bed-free" dessert with the following: 1 cup of sugar or xylitol with 2 tsp of cinnamon mixed together, then combined with 3 tbs of slightly melted butter. You want the butter to still be a bit cool so that it mixes in clumps. (This is what causes the "crumble" texture.)

8. Bake for 25 minutes.

Makes 4 portions

Pull this recipe out as a secret weapon for purpose of persuasion or reward. Apply as needed and make sure you have clean sheets on the bed. I have already put the sex back into rock n roll, I figure . . . **why stop with dessert?**

THEO'S VEGAN CHOCOLATE CAKE

Theo of LUNACHICKS, THEO & THE SKYSCRAPERS

This is not necessarily healthy, but it is vegan and delicious!

IN A BIG BOWL COMBINE:

- $1/2$ cup flour
- 1 cup sugar
- 3 heaping tbs of cocoa powder
- $1/2$ tsp salt
- 1 tsp baking soda
- 5 tbs canola oil
- 1 tbs white vinegar
- 1 cup cold water

1. Pre-heat oven to 350° F.

2. Mix well with a wooden spoon. Grease and flour an 8" x 8" pan.

3. Bake for 35 minutes.

Somewhat scientific explanation: The vinegar and baking soda with the water are what makes it rise. You won't taste the vinegar when it's done!

Yields 8 slices

SERVING SUGGESTION: Use whatever icing you like or raspberry jam on top, if you like the fruit/chocolate combo.

CHOCOLATE CHERRY CAKE AND FROSTING

Becca Manthe of THE TOSSERS

SEVERAL YEARS AGO, John Joseph and I were walking around the neighborhood. We walked past the Continental (when they still had shows!) and decided to stop in because Murphy's Law was headlining. There was an Irish-sounding punk band on stage, and I was floored. Their music was amazing, and I couldn't stop dancing. After they got off stage, I made it a point to meet the band. Over the years, I've continued to go to every one of their shows that I can. If they need help with merch, chances are you've seen me at some point behind their merch table. Becca plays violin and is amazingly talented. She's been veggie for years, so I reached out to her for a recipe. We got lucky, and she gave us her grandmother's recipe!

INGREDIENTS:

- 1 fudge cake mix (prepackaged)
- 1 can (21 oz) cherry pie filling
- 1 tsp almond extract
- 2 beaten eggs

1. Mix fudge cake mix, cherry pie filling, almond extract, and beaten eggs by hand and bake at 350 for 30-35 minutes in a greased 9" x 13" pan.

continued...

INGREDIENTS:

- 1 cup sugar
- 5 tbs butter/baking margarine
- $\frac{1}{2}$ cup milk
- $\frac{1}{3}$ package chocolate chips

1. Boil sugar, butter or baking margarine, and milk for 1 minute.

2. After removing from heat, stir in chocolate chips. Let frosting cool a while before using; it will thicken as it cools.

The last time I made this recipe I made mini cakes; you can also make cupcakes. The frosting is the best, very rich, and it sets quickly. If it sets before you've used it all, you can heat it back up on the stove; just be careful not to burn the chocolate. I have also substituted the milk with soy milk, and it still works. It has a different flavor, but it is still good.

If you want to get fancy, instead of using a fudge cake mix, you can substitute with any fudge cake recipe from scratch—you just have to cut back on some of the liquid because of the cherry pie filling. On the following page is a fudge cake recipe I used the last time I made this cake.

INGREDIENTS:

- 1 ½ cups sugar

- ½ cup cocoa

- 1 ½ tsp baking soda

- 2 cups flour

- ¾ tsp salt

- 1 ½ tsp vanilla

- ¾ cup vegetable oil

- 1 ½ cups water

- 1 ½ tsp vinegar

1. I made this as is. Just mix it all together in a bowl and add the cherries; skip all the other ingredients in the recipe using the box mix. It ends up being really moist, and there is no need to grease the pan if you do it from scratch.

It tastes the best after being refrigerated; after the frosting **completely** cools.

Yields 15 slices

SIMPLE DESSERT SAUCE

ms minx and friends

I CAN'T TAKE CREDIT FOR THIS ONE; I was at my friend Ames' house, cooking up a storm to impress my friends Laura and Bob. Ames, who is capable of cooking up a full meal for an army with a well-stocked kitchen, surprised me when she pulled out these two ingredients and told me to mix them together for the sauce for our fresh berries. I am now hooked on it, and would gladly eat a bowl of it with no berries—it's that good!

This is a simple sauce, **especially** good for fruits.

- All you need is sour cream and brown sugar.

Mix about 1½ tsp with a cup of sour cream.

That's it. **Enjoy!**

Makes about 1 cup

RESOURCES

BOOKS TAKE QUITE A LONG TIME to go to print and may also inhabit your bookshelf for many years to come.

It's for this reason we encourage you to visit:

www.PunkRockDomestics.com

On the pages of the site, you'll find product reviews, tips for getting things cheap, fun makeup and hair ideas, all sorts of tutorials from our members, expert advice areas, ways to do things on the lam, areas to post art, CD reviews—all sorts of good things.

This book has been inspired by those boards.

In addition, if you are a DIY fan, there are links to many of our members' stores, which I encourage you to check out!

NOTES